Tony Ferguson
weightloss programme

THE
Tony Ferguson
Cook Book

LOW GI GOOD-CARB RECIPES
FOR YOUR WELLBEING

Introduction From Tony

In 1997 my daughter Simone studied a course in Nutrition and never finished it because of the arrival of my grandson, Lawson. However, Simone convinced me that my daily food choices were pretty lousy at that time (I used to start my day on frankfurters for Pete's sake!). From that point on I knew there had to be a better way for my profession (Pharmacy) to help people change from poor to proper nutrition.

Our bodies were never meant to cope with FAST FOOD and its overload of high GI carbohydrates and trans fats. This unique book shows you in a simple way that there is another life…a life full of good-carbs and healthy nutritious food.

From my experience in the pharmacy, I know there are a variety of pills and potions available to help you lose weight. But the real secret to weight loss isn't through a prescription, it's through healthy and delicious food. This book will show you a range of delicious recipes that are easy to make and the whole family will enjoy. The aim of your journey through the Tony Ferguson Weightloss Programme is to get you to the stage where you don't need us any more. This cook book will certainly help you along the way.

Good food really tastes GOOD!

Enjoy the book and always remember that you cannot put a price on GOOD HEALTH.

Best wishes,

Tony Ferguson

Tony Ferguson PhC.MPS

"Most people have the perception that weight loss is boring and they'll get hungry…that need never be the case with this recipe book."

Contents

Using this book 4

The Glycemic Index 5

Eating for Health Conditions 6

Cooking the Healthy Way 7

Keeping Things Interesting 8

Beef 9

Chicken 21

Lamb 33

Pork 41

Seafood 47

Vegetarian 59

Side Dishes 71

Snacks 83

Sauces & Dressings 91

Index 95

Conversion Chart 96

Using This Book

This recipe book was designed to be used in conjunction with the Tony Ferguson Weightloss Programme. The Programme involves substituting our delicious soups, shakes and munch bars for two of your regular meals throughout the day. The third meal consists of protein and lots of fresh vegetables. Use this book to create something interesting!

Each of the recipes outlines the allowed protein serving for both males and females. The following table can be used as a general guide:

	MEAT, SEAFOOD & CHICKEN (RAW WEIGHT)	LOW FAT COTTAGE/ RICOTTA CHEESE & TOFU
Males	200-220g (palm size)	200-250g
Females	100-120g (palm size)	150g

Each recipe contains a nutritional analysis for both males and females based on the ingredients and relevant serving size of the dish. The following components are analysed:

ENERGY All foods contain energy and we need it to function. Different foods contain different amounts of energy and it is measured in kilojoules (kJ) and calories (cal).

PROTEIN Protein is measured in grams (g). It is important when losing weight to keep you full and make sure you maintain your muscle mass. Just watch your portion sizes.

FAT, SATURATED FAT Fat is measured in grams (g). It is high in energy so when trying to lose weight eat lean meats and cook foods by grilling, stir frying and barbecuing using olive oil spray.

CARBOHYDRATES Carbohydrates are measured in grams (g). Due to the low carbohydrate nature of the Programme it is important to keep your carbohydrates low. 90-150g of carbohydrates is the average daily intake while following the Programme.

SODIUM Sodium is measured in milligrams (mg). We recommend you keep your sodium intake below 2300mg/day and if you suffer high blood pressure try to stay below 1600mg/day.

CHOLESTEROL Cholesterol is measured in milligrams (mg). People with high cholesterol levels need to ensure they keep it to a minimum by avoiding saturated fats and eating good fats each day.

FIBRE Fibre is measured in grams (g). It is recommended that adults consume 25-30 grams of fibre per day. You will find it easier to reach these levels by taking Tony Ferguson Fibre in addition to consuming fresh fruits and vegetables to prevent constipation and promote bowel health.

Unless specified otherwise all vegetables and fruit are of a medium size when referred to in recipes.

The Glycemic Index

WHAT IS THE GLYCEMIC INDEX

The glycemic index (GI) ranks foods containing carbohydrate on a scale from 0 to 100 according to their ability to raise blood sugar levels.

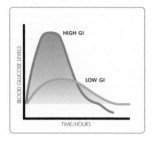

Foods with a high GI, 70 or above on the scale, are rapidly digested and absorbed and this causes a distinct rise and fall, or spike in blood sugar (glucose) levels (as seen in the graph). Alternatively, low GI foods with a value of less than 55 on the scale, are broken down slowly and produce a more gradual rise in blood sugar levels. Due to their slower rate of digestion, low GI foods enable you to feel fuller for longer while sustaining your energy levels throughout the day.

THE GLYCEMIC INDEX AND HEALTH

Insulin is a hormone secreted by the pancreas that allows glucose (sugar) to enter the cells and reduce blood sugar levels. The continuous consumption of high GI foods creates a large demand for insulin to reduce the blood sugar spiking and this can exhaust the pancreas and lead to diabetes. In the long term this can contribute to weight gain and heart disease.

There are many proven health benefits associated with adopting a low GI way of eating. They have been shown to improve blood glucose levels in people suffering from diabetes as well as playing a role in weight control by helping to manage appetite levels and delaying hunger.

The Tony Ferguson Weightloss Programme is based on the low GI principle. The sachets have a low GI of 22, and all the fresh fruits and vegetables recommended while following the Programme are low GI. This ensures that while losing weight you are also helping to regulate your blood sugar and energy levels so you look and feel great every day!

Eating for Health Conditions

HIGH BLOOD PRESSURE

By making a few simple changes to your diet you can help manage your blood pressure. Reducing salt has been proven to be one of the most effective methods of lowering high blood pressure. Salt provides our bodies with the minerals sodium and chlorine both of which are needed for normal function. The suggested adult intake for salt is no more than 6 grams per day. Salt is found in almost every food we eat, so you can easily get your daily requirements without adding any to your diet.

Tips for reducing sodium intake:
• Use fresh and dried herbs as well as spices to add flavour to your food
• Avoid adding salt to foods when cooking and use soy sauce sparingly
• Buy salt reduced or no added salt products when shopping for packaged foods

HIGH CHOLESTEROL

To manage high cholesterol levels you need to reduce your intake of saturated fats, which are found in animal and full fat dairy products, and increase your consumption of poly and monounsaturated fats found in nuts, avocados, olive oil and oily fish.

Tips for lowering cholesterol levels:
• Choose lean meats
• Use a small amount of rapeseed or olive oil when cooking
• Consume oily fish such as salmon or fresh tuna or try taking fish oil capsules
• Consume soluble fibre from Tony Ferguson Fibre, vegetables and fruits such as apples

TYPE 2 DIABETES

Nutrition plays an important role in the management of diabetes along with medication, exercise and monitoring of blood sugar levels.

There is a close relationship between the Glycemic Index and diabetes. It is scientifically proven that eating low GI foods helps control established diabetes because these foods produce lower blood glucose levels and therefore less insulin is required.

The Tony Ferguson Weightloss Programme is a low GI Programme which helps to stabilise blood sugar levels while providing adequate low GI carbohydrates in the form of fructose and lactose in the sachets.

Cooking the Healthy Way

Cooking healthy foods does not have to be difficult or time consuming. All it takes is a few simple changes to your daily routine to improve the quality of the food you eat.

The way you cook your food is an important aspect to consider when trying to lose weight. It is important that you retain the essential nutrients found in the foods while trying to keep the meal low calorie and most importantly ensuring it tastes great!

GRILLING Food is cooked on a wire rack so fat is able to drip away from the food. Ideal for thin cuts of meat and vegetables as it cooks quickly.

BARBECUING Involves food being cooked on a rack or a hotplate. This method requires little to no oil, depending on the food being cooked.

STIR FRYING A fast and healthy method of cooking especially if you use a non stick wok or frying pan with a little oil.

MICROWAVING No added fat and very little liquid is required which means it is a healthy way to cook and the food retains nutrients, colours and textures.

STEAMING Ideal for fish, chicken and vegetables. It is quick and requires no added fat while retaining the nutritional value of the foods.

TIPS TO REMEMBER FOR HEALTHY COOKING AT HOME
- Choose lean cuts of meat and poultry and remove all visible fat
- Reduce the amount of oil you use while cooking by spraying your food lightly with a good olive oil spray
- Avoid over-cooking vegetables as they lose much of their nutrition with heat. Try lightly steaming or microwaving rather than boiling to retain optimum nutrition
- Try stir frying foods in a small amount of salt reduced stock rather than oil

EXPERIMENTING WITH FLAVOURS
Healthy food need not be bland or tasteless. Try experimenting with different seasonings and you will soon begin to appreciate the lighter, fresher flavours they provide.
- Spices such as ginger, cumin, paprika and tumeric can spice up any dish
- Fresh or dried herbs will enhance the flavour of food
- Lemon or lime juice and zest give a fresh tangy taste
- A dash of red wine or balsamic vinegar will add a zesty flavour

Keeping Things Interesting

It is important that you try to keep your daily routine interesting as boredom is one of the most common reasons why people fail to stick to a weight loss programme. Why not try one of these great ideas!

HOT! HOT! HOT!

Try heating your favourite sachet flavour for a warm start to the day. It is especially good if you are missing your daily coffee, and the espresso, mocha or café latte flavours really hit the spot. Shake the contents of the sachet with at least 200ml of **cold** water in a shaker. Pour into a microwave safe mug and heat on high for 40 seconds.

SMOOTH AND CREAMY

For a creamy, custard-like dessert, shake your favourite sachet flavour with only 150ml of water in your shaker. Pour it into a small bowl and leave in the fridge for at least 40 minutes and you will be able to eat it with a spoon.

ICE CREAM

Mix your sachet with only 150ml of water in your shaker. Pour into a bowl and leave in the freezer for 40-90 minutes. It will set hard like an ice cream. Great for those hot summer days and tastes great with some diet jelly on the side!

WARM AND GOOEY!

This one is a real treat. For a pudding-like delight, mix your sachet with only 50ml of water in a ramekin to make a smooth paste. Heat in the microwave on high for 40 seconds and you will have your own warm pudding. The chocolate and mocha flavours make a great pudding.

REMEMBER THAT A SACHET IS A MEAL REGARDLESS OF HOW IT IS PREPARED.

DELICIOUS DINNERS

Select from over 30 different main meals, 10 side dishes and our range of different sauces and dressings in this book to spice up your evening meal.

SNACKS

For some healthy snack ideas to get you through the day check out the section starting on page 83.

ALCOHOL

If you enjoy a glass of wine with a nice meal, you are in luck! Selected alcohol beverages are available as a Treat option on the Tony Ferguson Weightloss Programme; just remember these may be consumed only once or twice a week. Dry red or white wines are your best choices. Speak to your Tony Ferguson Weightloss Practitioner for a full range of Treat options.

Beef

Beef is a rich source of both protein and iron but unfortunately it can also contain saturated fats. For this reason ensure that you trim all visible fats from the meat before cooking and choose lean cuts such as fillet steak. It is recommended that you eat red meat no more than 2 to 3 times per week.

Burritos

Serves 4

INGREDIENTS

1 tablespoon olive oil
2 cloves garlic, crushed
1 medium onion, diced
4 x 120g lean beef mince (females)
4 x 220g lean beef mince (males)
1 medium red pepper, diced
1 red chilli, thinly sliced
2 medium tomatoes, diced finely
1 tablespoon tomato pureé
1 cup salt reduced beef stock
8 large iceberg lettuce leaves, washed and dried
1 avocado, diced
4 tablespoons tomato salsa

METHOD

1. Heat the oil in a large pan or wok on high and add the garlic and onions and cook until soft. Add the mince and stir until cooked and brown.
2. Add the red pepper, chilli, half the tomato, tomato pureé and stock, reduce the heat and simmer for 5 to 10 minutes, stirring occasionally until the sauce thickens.
3. Spoon the mince mixture evenly into the lettuce cups and top with remaining diced tomato, avocado cubes and salsa.

PER SERVING

AVERAGE QUANTITY	FEMALES	MALES
energy	414cal	601cal
protein	37.9g	65.5g
fat / saturated	25.1g / 7.4g	33.5g / 11.1g
cholesterol	88mg	161mg
carbohydrates	7.1g	7.1g
fibre	3.7g	3.7g
sodium	444mg	503mg

Moroccan Minted Beef

Serves 4

INGREDIENTS

2 tablespoons olive oil
4 x 120g lean beef strips (females)
4 x 220g lean beef strips (males)
1 medium onion, sliced
1 teaspoon cumin
½ teaspoon nutmeg
½ teaspoon ground ginger
1 tablespoon grated lemon rind
400g can crushed tomatoes
2 tablespoons mint leaves

METHOD

1. Heat the oil in a frying pan over high heat and cook the beef strips until browned, remove from the pan.
2. To the pan add the onion and cook for 2-3 minutes. Add the spices and lemon rind and cook for 1 minute. Add tomatoes and simmer until slightly thickened, stirring occasionally.
3. Return the beef to the pan and cook until heated through.
4. Serve sprinkled with fresh mint.

Serving suggestion: Serve with a side of steamed vegetables.

PER SERVING

AVERAGE QUANTITY	FEMALES	MALES
energy	328cal	507cal
protein	36.2g	65.2g
fat / saturated	17.6g / 5g	24.5g / 8.1g
cholesterol	84mg	154mg
carbohydrates	4.8g	4.8g
fibre	2g	2g
sodium	88mg	146mg

Steak with Onion Salsa

Serves 4

INGREDIENTS

2 large red onions, thickly sliced
2 ripe tomatoes, halved
½ bunch flat leaf parsley, roughly chopped
10 fresh basil leaves
1 tablespoon balsamic vinegar
2 tablespoons extra virgin olive oil
Salt and freshly ground black pepper
4 × 120g lean beef steak (females)
4 × 220g lean beef steak (males)

METHOD

1. On a heated, oiled barbecue plate grill the onion and tomato cut side down until blackened on both sides. Remove from heat, roughly chop and place in a bowl.
2. To the bowl add parsley, basil, balsamic vinegar and oil and season with salt and freshly ground pepper. Toss until combined.
3. Cook steaks on hot barbecue plate until done as desired. Remove from heat and let rest for 2 minutes.
4. Serve steak topped with onion salsa, extra parsley and a fresh green salad or a serve of Notatoes (see page 73 for Notatoes recipe).

Tip: For extra flavour try adding fresh chilli or ground cumin to the salsa before serving.

PER SERVING

AVERAGE QUANTITY	FEMALES	MALES
energy	320cal	497cal
protein	33.8g	60.7g
fat / saturated	18.3g / 5.4g	25.9g / 8.8g
cholesterol	90mg	165mg
carbohydrates	4g	4g
fibre	1.6g	1.6g
sodium	79mg	152mg

Steak Sandwich Serves 4

INGREDIENTS

Olive oil spray
2 medium aubergines cut into thick slices lengthways
1 large red pepper, seeds removed and quartered
1 cup mushrooms, thinly sliced
4 x 120g lean beef steak (females)
4 x 220g lean beef steak (males)

1 large onion, thinly sliced
100g baby rocket leaves
1 teaspoon olive oil
1 tablespoon balsamic vinegar
Hot English mustard

METHOD

1. Heat barbecue. Lightly spray aubergines and pepper with olive oil and cook on the grill until tender. At the same time, on the hotplate side cook mushrooms and onions until soft.

2. Lightly spray steaks with oil and cook on grill until done as desired, turning once during cooking.

3. Prepare rocket salad by adding rocket, oil and vinegar in a bowl. Toss to combine and set aside.

4. To serve place a slice of aubergine on the plate. Top with pepper and steak. Spread a small amount of mustard on the steak and top with grilled onion and mushroom. Place another slice of aubergine on top of the stack and serve with the rocket salad on the side.

PER SERVING

AVERAGE QUANTITY	FEMALES	MALES
energy	339cal	516cal
protein	39.1g	66g
fat / saturated	13g / 4.4g	20.6g / 7.8g
cholesterol	90mg	165mg
carbohydrates	11.9g	11.9g
fibre	9.3g	9.3g
sodium	134mg	187mg

Hearty Beef Casserole Serves 4

INGREDIENTS

1 tablespoon olive oil

2 small onions, cut into wedges

2 cloves garlic, crushed

4 x 120g lean chuck steak, cubed (females)

4 x 220g lean chuck steak, cubed (males)

2 cups salt reduced beef stock

400g can diced tomatoes

1 carrot, sliced

3 sticks of celery, sliced

1 teaspoon cumin

1 teaspoon coriander

2 button squash, quartered (optional)

METHOD

1. Preheat oven to 160°C.

2. Heat the oil in a heatproof casserole dish, over medium heat. Cook the onion and garlic until soft. Remove from dish and set aside.

3. Heat casserole dish on high. Season the beef with salt and pepper, add half to the dish and cook until brown. Remove and repeat with remaining beef.

4. To the empty dish, add the stock and bring to the boil. Return onion, garlic and beef to dish then add the tomatoes, carrots, celery and spices.

5. Return to the boil, cover and place in the preheated oven for 1 hour.

6. Remove, add squash and return to oven to cook for a further 30 minutes.

7. Serve with Notatoes (cauliflower mash) according to recipe on page 73.

PER SERVING

AVERAGE QUANTITY	FEMALES	MALES
energy	310cal	485cal
protein	38.5g	66.4g
fat / saturated	13.3g / 4.3g	20.2g / 7.2g
cholesterol	83mg	152mg
carbohydrates	7.3g	7.3g
fibre	3.2g	3.2g
sodium	624mg	690mg

Shepherd's Pie

Serves 4

INGREDIENTS

1 tablespoon olive oil
4 x 120g lean beef mince (females)
4 x 220g lean beef mince (males)
1 teaspoon crushed garlic
1 large onion, diced
½ teaspoon cumin
400g can diced tomatoes
1 teaspoon dried mixed herbs
1 cup prepared gravy (from suggested list)*
100g green beans, trimmed and chopped
2 sticks of celery, sliced thinly
1 carrot, peeled and diced
Notatoes (see page 73)

METHOD

1. Heat oil in pan and add mince, garlic, onion and cumin and cook until mince is browned.
2. Add the tomatoes, mixed herbs and gravy and combine well. Add the chopped vegetables, reduce the heat and simmer for 10 minutes until sauce thickens and the vegetables are soft.
3. Make Notatoes (cauliflower mash) according to recipe on page 73.
4. Pre heat the grill to medium-high. Transfer the mince mixture to an oven proof dish and top with the Notatoes. Place dish under the grill until the top is lightly browned.

Serving suggestion: Serve immediately with freshly steamed vegetables and salt and pepper.

PER SERVING

AVERAGE QUANTITY	FEMALES	MALES
energy	382cal	569cal
protein	39.3g	66.9g
fat / saturated	18.4g / 7.1g	26.8g / 10.8g
cholesterol	97mg	170mg
carbohydrates	11.9g	11.9g
fibre	6g	6g
sodium	623mg	682mg

When using packaged goods check the nutrition label. It must be under 5g carbohydrates per serving.

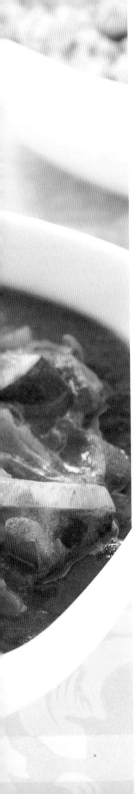

Rich Beef Curry

Serves 4

INGREDIENTS

1 tablespoon olive oil
4 x 120g beef (females)
4 x 220g beef (males)
2 tablespoons garam masala
1 teaspoon tumeric
1 teaspoon cumin
2 red chillies, finely chopped
1 medium onion, sliced
1 teaspoon of grated fresh ginger
2 cloves garlic, crushed
1 tablespoon tomato pureé
2 small tomatoes, diced
400g can crushed tomatoes
1 small courgette, halved lengthways and sliced
½ red pepper, seeded and diced
1 cup salt reduced beef stock
Fresh coriander to garnish

METHOD

1. Heat oil on high in large frying pan or wok and cook beef, spices and chilli until beef is browned all over. Add onion, ginger and garlic and cook until soft.
2. Stir in tomato pureé and fresh and canned tomatoes until well combined then add the other vegetables followed by the stock. Bring to the boil then reduce the heat and simmer for 20 minutes, covered until the beef is tender.

Serving suggestion: Serve on a bed of cauliflower rice according to recipe on page 74, garnished with freshly chopped coriander.

PER SERVING

AVERAGE QUANTITY	FEMALES	MALES
energy	327cal	515cal
protein	38g	66.3g
fat / saturated	14.9g / 5g	23.1g / 8.6g
cholesterol	83mg	152mg
carbohydrates	8.1g	8.1g
fibre	3.5g	3.5g
sodium	336mg	389mg

Spicy Meatballs Serves 4

INGREDIENTS

4 x 120g lean beef mince (females)
4 x 220g lean beef mince (males)
1 tablespoon fresh ginger, grated
2 tablespoons fresh coriander, chopped
1 tablespoon soy sauce
½ red pepper, finely diced
½ green pepper, finely diced

½ carrot, grated
1 egg, lightly beaten
1 clove garlic, finely chopped
1 teaspoon fish sauce
1 medium red chilli, seeded and finely diced
2 tablespoons olive oil
500g jar tomato pasta sauce or see recipe page 93.

METHOD

1. Place all ingredients, except oil and tomato pasta sauce in a large bowl and mix well until combined. Form the mixture into small round balls. Place on a baking tray and refrigerate for 1 hour.
2. Heat the oil in a large frying pan and cook the meatballs in batches, for 5-6 minutes or until brown and cooked through.
3. Once cooked, return all meatballs to the pan and add the tomato sauce; cook until the sauce is heated through.
4. Divide meatballs between serving plates, sprinkle with fresh basil and serve with a garden salad.

PER SERVING

AVERAGE QUANTITY	FEMALES	MALES
energy	385cal	572cal
protein	37.7g	65.3g
fat / saturated	20.9g / 6.2g	29.3g / 9.9g
cholesterol	141mg	214mg
carbohydrates	9.6g	9.6g
fibre	3.2g	3.2g
sodium	792mg	852mg

When using packaged goods check the nutrition label. It must be under 5g carbohydrates per serving.

Chicken

Gram for gram skinless chicken is one of the lowest fat meats you can choose. It is high in protein and iron as well as other essential vitamins and minerals. Although the white breast meat has the lowest fat content, the darker meat such as the thigh is still a healthy option. To keep the calories low remember to remove all skin and visible fat before cooking.

Lemon Spice Chicken with Crunchy Cabbage Salad

Serves 4

INGREDIENTS

4 x 120g chicken thigh pieces (females)
4 x 220g chicken thigh pieces (males)
Olive oil spray
2 teaspoons paprika (smoky paprika is best)
½ teaspoon lemon pepper
½ teaspoon dried oregano
¼ teaspoon cayenne pepper
½ teaspoon salt

CRUNCHY CABBAGE SALAD

¼ red cabbage finely shredded
1 large carrot, peeled and sliced into thin batons
2 shallots, sliced
1 cucumber, seeded and cut into batons
2 tablespoons lemon juice
1 tablespoon white wine vinegar
1 tablespoon olive oil

METHOD

1. Preheat oven to 200°C.
2. Line a baking tray with foil. Lightly spray chicken with olive oil.
3. Combine all dry ingredients in a large snap lock bag. Add chicken and toss until it is well coated.
4. Place the chicken onto the baking tray and bake for 30-35 minutes or until chicken is cooked through. When cold enough to handle, finely slice.
5. Combine with crunchy cabbage salad.

TO MAKE THE SALAD

1. Place all ingredients in a large bowl.
2. Whisk lemon juice, vinegar and oil together in a small jug and drizzle over salad. Toss to combine.

PER SERVING

AVERAGE QUANTITY	FEMALES	MALES
energy	340cal	556cal
protein	32.1g	57.5g
fat / saturated	21.1g / 5.2g	33.9g / 9g
cholesterol	163mg	299mg
carbohydrates	3.7g	3.7g
fibre	3g	3g
sodium	453mg	559mg

Creamy Coconut Curry

Serves 4

INGREDIENTS

1 tablespoon olive oil
1 small onion, sliced thinly
1 clove garlic, crushed
4 x 120g lean chicken breast sliced (females)
4 x 220g lean chicken breast sliced (males)
1 teaspoon curry powder
2 tablespoons smooth low fat ricotta cheese
2 drops of coconut cooking essence
2 cups salt reduced chicken stock
100g green beans, trimmed and halved
100g mange tout, trimmed and halved
1 red pepper, seeded and sliced thinly
½ cup fresh coriander, roughly chopped
1 cup bean sprouts

METHOD

1. Heat oil in a wok on high heat. Add half the onion, garlic and half the chicken. Stir fry for 2-3 minutes until browned. Remove from wok and repeat with remaining chicken.
2. To the empty wok add the curry powder, low fat ricotta, coconut essence and stock. Stir together and bring to the boil. Reduce the heat and simmer until sauce thickens, about 10 minutes.
3. Return the chicken mixture to the wok and add the beans, mange tout and the red pepper. Simmer for 4-5 minutes until the chicken is cooked through.
4. Remove from heat and stir in coriander and bean sprouts.

Serving suggestion: Serve on its own or on a bed of cauliflower rice (according to recipe on page 74), topped with extra bean sprouts and coriander.

PER SERVING

AVERAGE QUANTITY	FEMALES	MALES
energy	327cal	502cal
protein	37.2g	62.9g
fat / saturated	16.5g / 4.6g	24.5g / 6.9g
cholesterol	107mg	190mg
carbohydrates	5.8g	5.8g
fibre	2.8g	2.8g
sodium	457mg	540mg

Chicken Coriander Serves 4

INGREDIENTS

4 × 120g lean chicken breast pieces (females)
4 × 220g lean chicken breast pieces (males)
2 tablespoons olive oil
¼ cup coriander leaves, chopped finely
Juice and grated rind from a medium lemon
   (save 1 tablespoon for dressing)
2 cloves garlic, crushed
1 teaspoon cumin
½ teaspoon paprika

SALAD

100g baby spinach leaves
2 large ripe tomatoes, roughly chopped
1 Spanish onion, sliced
2 tablespoons fresh mint
1 tablespoon fresh lemon juice
1 teaspoon olive oil
Black pepper

METHOD

1. Preheat oven to 180°C.
2. Make small diagonal cuts in the chicken flesh and lay the chicken in a single layer in a shallow baking dish.
3. Combine oil, coriander, lemon juice & rind, garlic and spices in a bowl and mix to combine, Pour mixture over the chicken and toss until each piece is evenly coated. Leave to marinate for 30 minutes.
4. Bake in the oven for 25-30 minutes or until chicken is fully cooked.
5. Slice chicken and serve with baby spinach salad.

TO MAKE SALAD

Combine all salad ingredients in a large bowl and toss.

PER SERVING

AVERAGE QUANTITY	FEMALES	MALES
energy	334cal	510cal
protein	32.8g	58.4g
fat / saturated	20.1g / 4.2g	28g / 6.5g
cholesterol	100mg	183mg
carbohydrates	3.8g	3.8g
fibre	2.5g	2.5g
sodium	114mg	197mg

Spiced Chicken Skewers Serves 4

INGREDIENTS

½ cup lemon juice
2 tablespoons olive oil
1 teaspoon sweetener
2 cloves garlic, crushed
2 teaspoons ground cumin
1 teaspoon ground tumeric
¼ teaspoon ground cinnamon
½ teaspoon cayenne pepper
4 × 120g lean chicken tenderloin pieces
 (females)

4 × 220g lean chicken tenderloin pieces
 (males)
Olive oil cooking spray
100g coral lettuce, washed and dried
1 avocado, stone removed and sliced thinly
Ground black pepper
1 tablespoon white wine vinegar
1 tablespoon olive oil

METHOD

1. Soak 8-12 wooden skewers in water for 30 minutes.
2. Mix lemon juice, olive oil, sweetener, garlic, spices
and pepper in a small bowl to form a smooth paste.
3. Thread each chicken tenderloin onto a wooden
skewer. Coat each tenderloin with the marinade and
place in the refrigerator for 30 minutes to allow the
flavours to develop.
4. Heat a grill plate and spray lightly with olive oil spray.
Cook each of the chicken skewers for 3 minutes each
side or until chicken is cooked through.
5. Combine lettuce, avocado, pepper, vinegar and olive
oil. Toss. Serve with chicken skewers.

PER SERVING

AVERAGE QUANTITY	FEMALES	MALES
energy	461cal	648cal
protein	35.1g	63.2g
fat / saturated	34.5g / 6.9g	42.5g / 9.2g
cholesterol	108mg	198mg
carbohydrates	1.4g	1.4g
fibre	1.3g	1.3g
sodium	112mg	199mg

Simply Chicken Schnitzel

Serves 4

INGREDIENTS

4 x 120g lean chicken breast pieces (females)
4 x 220g lean chicken breast pieces (males)
1 large egg
½-1 cup of Tony Ferguson Fibre
1 teaspoon dried oregano or mixed herbs
½ teaspoon paprika
Salt and pepper
2 tablespoons olive oil
500g broccoli, cut into florets
1 large carrot, peeled, cut into ribbons
1 fresh lemon, halved
Freshly ground black pepper

METHOD

1. Pre-heat oven to 180°C.
2. Place each chicken breast between 2 plastic freezer bags and pound until chicken is 1cm thick. Trim any loose edges.
3. Place the egg in a small bowl and beat lightly with a fork. Set aside. Combine Tony Ferguson Fibre, dried herbs, paprika and salt and pepper in a medium sized bowl and toss to combine.
4. Dip each piece of chicken, first in the egg, then in the Tony Ferguson Fibre mixture until well coated. Refrigerate for 30 minutes.
5. Heat the oil in a large frying pan over high heat. Pan fry until golden then bake in the oven for 5-10 mins or until cooked.
6. Steam broccoli and carrot until tender. Place in a large stainless steel bowl and add the juice from half the lemon and some pepper. Toss.
7. Serve chicken schnitzel with a wedge of fresh lemon and the vegetables.

Serving suggestion: For a flavour variation try serving the schnitzel with Notatoes (according to the recipe on page 73) and your favourite low carb gravy (when using packaged goods it must be under 5g carbohydrates per serving).

Tip: Broccoli should be cooked for as short a time as possible – ideally just a few minutes. Steaming is the best method followed by boiling in a small amount of water. Broccoli is a good source of folic acid, which promotes the production of serotonin, a mood enhancing chemical produced naturally within the body. So eat your broccoli and smile!

PER SERVING

AVERAGE QUANTITY	FEMALES	MALES
energy	410cal	595cal
protein	42.8g	70.9g
fat / saturated	21.1g / 4.6g	29.1g / 6.9g
cholesterol	163mg	253mg
carbohydrates	11.9g	11.9g
fibre	13.8g	13.8g
sodium	156mg	243mg

Balsamic Chicken

Serves 4

INGREDIENTS

2 tablespoons balsamic vinegar
1 clove garlic, crushed
2 tablespoons extra virgin olive oil
4 x 120g lean chicken breast pieces (females)
4 x 220g lean chicken breast pieces (males)
1 cup of button mushrooms, sliced
1 cup salt reduced chicken stock
2 teaspoons fresh thyme leaves
1 tablespoon fresh chopped parsley
1 cup broccoli florets
1 cup cauliflower florets
1 small courgette sliced

METHOD

1. Combine balsamic vinegar, garlic and 1 tablespoon of oil and mix. Coat each chicken breast in the vinegar mixture.
2. Heat 1 tablespoon of oil in a large frying pan. Cook chicken for 3 minutes each side. Remove chicken from the pan.
3. Add mushrooms to the pan and cook for 2 minutes until soft. Add stock and bring to the boil. Simmer until reduced by half. Return chicken to the pan until heated through and stir through herbs.
4. Steam vegetables and serve with chicken, mushrooms and sauce.

PER SERVING

AVERAGE QUANTITY	FEMALES	MALES
energy	335cal	511cal
protein	35.6g	61.2g
fat / saturated	19.7g / 4.3g	27.7g / 6.6g
cholesterol	100mg	183mg
carbohydrates	2.6g	2.6g
fibre	3.2g	3.2g
sodium	271mg	360mg

Chicken with Oven Roasted Tomatoes

Serves 4

INGREDIENTS

4 Italian tomatoes, halved
2 tablespoons olive oil
Salt and pepper
1 teaspoon dried oregano
4 x 120g lean chicken breast pieces (females)
4 x 220g lean chicken breast pieces (males)
1 clove garlic, crushed
½ teaspoon of paprika
1 teaspoon of thyme
½ cup salt reduced chicken stock
¼ teaspoon chilli flakes
250g asparagus, steamed
1 lemon rind, grated

METHOD

1. Preheat oven to 180°C.
2. Place tomatoes cut side up on a baking tray and drizzle with olive oil. Season with salt, pepper and dried oregano and bake for 30-35 minutes.
3. Cook chicken in a lightly oiled pan for 10-15 minutes or until cooked through.
4. At the same time place garlic, paprika, thyme, chicken stock and chilli flakes in a small saucepan over high heat. Bring to the boil then reduce to a simmer and leave for 8-10 minutes or until the liquid has reduced by half.
5. Divide the steamed asparagus between each plate, top with the chicken and two tomato halves. Drizzle with the warm chilli dressing.
6. Garnish with extra lemon rind.

PER SERVING

AVERAGE QUANTITY	FEMALES	MALES
energy	309cal	471cal
protein	32.6g	57.2g
fat / saturated	17.7g / 3.7g	24.7g / 5.7g
cholesterol	95mg	174mg
carbohydrates	3.5g	3.5g
fibre	2.3g	2.3g
sodium	186mg	262mg

Cajun Chicken and Avocado Salad Serves 4

INGREDIENTS

4 x 120g lean chicken breast pieces (females)
4 x 220g lean chicken breast pieces (males)

CAJUN SEASONING

1 tablespoon dried basil
1 tablespoon paprika
1 teaspoon dried garlic powder
2 teaspoons cayenne pepper
½ teaspoon dried oregano
½ teaspoon dried parsley
½ teaspoon dried thyme

AVOCADO SALAD

1 cup baby rocket
1 cup watercress
1 punnet cherry tomatoes, halved
2 shallots, thinly sliced
100g mange tout, blanched and halved
100g button mushrooms, thinly sliced
1 avocado, stone removed, peeled and cubed
French or Italian dressing (recipes on page 94)

METHOD

1. Mix all ingredients for Cajun seasoning in a small bowl until combined. Rub the seasoning over each of the pieces of chicken breast until well coated.
2. Cook chicken in a large lightly oiled frying pan until cooked through. Slice the chicken into 1-2 cm thick slices and serve over the avocado salad.

TO MAKE SALAD

Combine all ingredients in a large bowl and toss. Top with 1 tablespoon of French or Italian dressing.

PER SERVING

AVERAGE QUANTITY	FEMALES	MALES
energy	500cal	685cal
protein	37.4g	66.5g
fat / saturated	36.6g / 7.3g	44.6g / 9.6g
cholesterol	108mg	198mg
carbohydrates	4g	4g
fibre	3.7g	3.7g
sodium	321mg	408 mg

Tip: Avocado has a high fat content but most of its fats are actually beneficial to the body. It is particularly high in omega-6 fats that stabilise blood sugar levels and keep hunger at bay.

Lamb

Lamb is especially rich in iron, zinc and the B group vitamins. It contains similar amounts of saturated fats to other red meats, and due to the fact lamb is leaner than ever, it is an appropriate source of protein. Choose cuts such as lean leg steak and cook with as little added fat as possible to control the calories.

Balsamic Lamb with Asparagus Salad

Serves 4

INGREDIENTS

4 x 120g trim lamb leg steaks (females)
4 x 220g trim lamb leg steaks (males)
1 lemon
2 tablespoons olive oil
2 tablespoons balsamic vinegar
2 bunches asparagus, woody ends removed,
    cut diagonally into thirds
100g baby spinach leaves

METHOD

1. Preheat oven to 200°C.
2. Place lamb steaks in a non stick oven proof dish. Cut lemon into slices and arrange over the top of the lamb. Combine oil and balsamic vinegar and drizzle half over the lamb. Roast for 15 minutes.
3. Toss asparagus in the remaining oil and vinegar mixture, add to the lamb dish and roast for a further 10 minutes. Remove lamb and allow to rest for 5 minutes.
4. Toss asparagus and spinach together and divide between serving plates. Thinly slice lamb steaks and add to salad.

PER SERVING

AVERAGE QUANTITY	FEMALES	MALES
energy	315cal	494cal
protein	36g	64.4g
fat / saturated	17.8g / 5.4g	24.9g / 8.8g
cholesterol	110mg	202mg
carbohydrates	1.1g	1.1g
fibre	1.7g	1.7g
sodium	86mg	152mg

Lemon and Garlic Lamb Rack

Serves 4

INGREDIENTS

1 tablespoon lemon juice
1 tablespoon olive oil
1 clove garlic, crushed
1 tablespoon freshly chopped rosemary
1 French trimmed lamb rack – 8 cutlets
  (females 2-3 cutlets)
1½ French trimmed lamb rack – 12 cutlets
  (males 3-4 cutlets)
2 lemons, cut into wedges
1 Spanish onion, cut into wedges
500g green beans, trimmed
2 teaspoons seeded mustard
1 tablespoon white wine vinegar

METHOD

1. Preheat oven to 180°C. Combine lemon juice, oil, garlic and chopped rosemary to form a paste. Pour the paste over the lamb rack and leave to marinate for at least 1 hour.
2. Place lemon wedges, onion and some extra rosemary sprigs in the bottom of a baking dish and place lamb rack on top making sure to add any extra marinade from the dish. Bake in a hot oven for 35-40 minutes.
3. Steam beans until tender and combine in a stainless steel bowl with mustard and white wine vinegar and toss until beans are well coated. Serve cutlets with the bean salad.

PER SERVING

AVERAGE QUANTITY	FEMALES	MALES
energy	336cal	543cal
protein	35.4g	62.8g
fat / saturated	18g / 7.4g	28.7g / 13g
cholesterol	131mg	240mg
carbohydrates	4.9g	4.9g
fibre	4.7g	4.7g
sodium	140mg	234mg

Rosemary Lamb Steaks with Ratatouille

Serves 4

INGREDIENTS

4 x 120g trim lamb steaks (females)
4 x 220g trim lamb steaks (males)
1 tablespoon dried rosemary
Salt and pepper
Olive oil spray
RATATOUILLE
1 aubergine, cut into 2cm cubes
Salt
1 teaspoon olive oil
1 red onion, diced
1 garlic clove, crushed
2 courgettes, diced
1 red pepper, seeded and diced into 2cm pieces
400g can crushed tomatoes
1 cup water
½ cup fresh basil, roughly chopped

METHOD

TO MAKE RATATOUILLE
1. Place aubergine cubes in a colander and sprinkle with salt. Leave for 30 minutes and drain.
2. Heat oil in a large pan, add onion, garlic and cook until tender. Add all other vegetables and cook, stirring for 2 minutes. Add tomatoes, water and basil. Reduce the heat and simmer for 45 minutes until all vegetables are cooked.

TO COOK LAMB
1. Sprinkle each lamb steak with rosemary, salt and pepper and spray with olive oil. Set aside.
2. Scar meat 3 minutes each side on barbecue plate or grill.
3. Put into lined baking dish and top with half the ratatouille.
4. Bake for 5-10 minutes or until cooked to your liking.
5. Rest for 10 minutes and serve with the remaining ratatouille.

Tip: The ratatouille flavour develops with time, so make it the day before and reheat gently.

PER SERVING

AVERAGE QUANTITY	FEMALES	MALES
energy	309cal	489cal
protein	40.4g	70.9g
fat / saturated	10.3g / 3.4g	16.5g / 6.1g
cholesterol	110mg	202mg
carbohydrates	10.3g	10.3g
fibre	6g	6g
sodium	128mg	209mg

Lamb and Mint Salad   Serves 4

INGREDIENTS

1 tablespoon olive oil
4 x 120g trim lamb leg steaks (females)
4 x 220g trim lamb leg steaks (males)
Salt and pepper
200g green beans, blanched
½ punnet cherry tomatoes, halved

100g rocket leaves
¼ cup mint leaves

MINT DRESSING
¼ cup mint leaves, chopped
¼ cup extra virgin olive oil
2 tablespoons red wine vinegar

METHOD

1. Heat the oil in a non stick frying pan over high heat.
Season the lamb with salt and pepper and seal on both
sides. Reduce heat to medium and cook for a further
2-3 minutes. Set aside to rest.
2. In a large bowl place beans, tomatoes, rocket and
mint. Slice the lamb into thin strips and add to the
bowl. Toss gently.
3. Distribute between serving plates and drizzle with
mint dressing.

MINT DRESSING

Whisk together the oil and the vinegar, season with salt
and pepper and stir in the mint.

PER SERVING

AVERAGE QUANTITY	FEMALES	MALES
energy	414cal	592cal
protein	36g	64.3g
fat / saturated	27.7g / 6.7g	34.8g / 10.1g
cholesterol	110mg	202mg
carbohydrates	3.5g	3.5g
fibre	3.3g	3.3g
sodium	111mg	177mg

Pork

Pork is a nutrient-dense meat and is one of the best sources of B group vitamins, particularly thiamine. This lean meat contains only a small amount more fat than beef and although it has a relatively high amount of cholesterol, once the external fat is removed it is comparable to other lower calorie protein sources.

Lemon Sage Pork Cutlets

Serves 4

IINGREDIENTS

4 x 120g lean pork cutlets (females)
4 x 220g lean pork cutlets (males)
½ cup sage leaves
2 tablespoons olive oil
2 tablespoons lemon juice
1 tablespoon lemon rind

Ground pepper
1 cucumber, thinly sliced
100g watercress
2 tablespoons lemon juice
Salt and pepper

METHOD

1. Place cutlets in a shallow dish. Finely chop half of the sage and add the oil, lemon juice and rind and pepper in a jug. Whisk to combine. Pour over cutlets and refrigerate for 1 hour.
2. Heat a non stick frying pan over high heat. Remove cutlets from marinade, reserving marinade, and cook for 3-5 minutes each side until cooked through. Set aside.
3. Add remaining marinade and sage leaves to the hot frying pan and cook for 2-3 minutes until sage is crisp.
4. Combine cucumber, watercress, lemon juice, salt and pepper and toss.
5. Serve the cutlets on a bed of cucumber salad, top with crispy sage and warm dressing.

PER SERVING

AVERAGE QUANTITY	FEMALES	MALES
energy	324cal	514cal
protein	37.2g	67.4g
fat / saturated	18.3g / 4.7g	25.7g / 7.7g
cholesterol	109mg	200mg
carbohydrates	1.3g	1.3g
fibre	1.4g	1.4g
sodium	119mg	198mg

Pork Chops with Chargrilled Vegetable Salad

Serves 4

INGREDIENTS

Olive oil spray
4 x 120g pork cutlets, fat trimmed (females)
4 x 220g pork cutlets, fat trimmed (males)
1 red pepper, seeded
1 green pepper, seeded

1 large courgette, sliced lengthways and halved
6 large brown mushrooms, quartered
1 tablespoon balsamic vinegar
100g rocket leaves

METHOD

1. Heat a grill plate and spray with olive oil.
Cook pork cutlets for 3 minutes each side.
Set aside.
2. Cook the vegetables on a heated, oiled grill plate for
2-5 minutes each side until tender and slightly charred.
Combine in a large bowl with half the balsamic vinegar
and rocket leaves. Toss to coat.
3. Serve pork cutlets with salad and a drizzle of the
remaining balsamic vinegar.

PER SERVING

AVERAGE QUANTITY	FEMALES	MALES
energy	269cal	458cal
protein	39g	69.1g
fat / saturated	10.7g / 3.6g	18.2g / 6.5g
cholesterol	109mg	200mg
carbohydrates	2.8g	2.8g
fibre	2.2g	2.2g
sodium	107mg	186mg

Mustard Pork with Warm Tomato Salad

Serves 4

INGREDIENTS

1 tablespoon olive oil
1 tablespoon wholegrain mustard
2 garlic cloves, crushed
4 x 120g trim pork steaks (females)
4 x 220g trim pork steaks (males)
Olive oil spray
3 Italian tomatoes, quartered
100g baby spinach leaves
100g green beans, blanched, halved
1 small Spanish onion, sliced thinly
1 tablespoon red wine vinegar

METHOD

1. Combine oil, mustard and garlic in a small bowl. Coat each pork steak in the mustard paste.
2. Heat a large frying pan and spray with olive oil. Cook steaks for 3-5 minutes each side.
3. Heat a grill to high. Spray tomatoes with olive oil, and place under the grill for 5-10 minutes. Remove from heat and combine in a large bowl with spinach, onion, beans and vinegar. Toss gently.
4. Distribute salad between serving plates and top with warm pork steak.

PER SERVING

AVERAGE QUANTITY	FEMALES	MALES
energy	285cal	452cal
protein	39.1g	69.7g
fat / saturated	11.6g / 2.8g	16.4g / 4.6g
cholesterol	103mg	189mg
carbohydrates	3.8g	3.8g
fibre	3.3g	3.3g
sodium	126mg	186mg

Asian Pork Salad Serves 4

INGREDIENTS

4 x 120g trim pork fillets (females)
4 x 220g trim pork fillets (males)
1 teaspoon Chinese five spice seasoning
Olive oil spray
1 bunch baby pak choi, finely shredded
½ Chinese cabbage, finely shredded
1 carrot, peeled, cut into matchsticks

1 red pepper, seeded and finely sliced
1 cup bean sprouts
1 cup finely shredded mint
1 tablespoon fresh lemon or lime juice
1 tablespoon soy sauce
2 teaspoons sweetener
1 teaspoon sesame oil

METHOD

1. Sprinkle pork with Chinese five spice. Spray a large frying pan with olive oil and place over medium heat. Cook pork for 4-5 minutes each side. Remove from heat and rest for 10 minutes.
2. Place pak choi, Chinese cabbage, carrot, the red pepper, bean sprouts and mint in a bowl and toss.
3. Combine lemon or lime juice, soy sauce, sweetener and sesame oil in a screw top jar and shake until mixed.
4. Thinly slice pork across the grain and add to the salad, drizzle with dressing, toss and serve immediately.

PER SERVING

AVERAGE QUANTITY	FEMALES	MALES
energy	302cal	492cal
protein	39.5g	69.7g
fat / saturated	13.5g / 4.2g	21g / 7.1g
cholesterol	111mg	202mg
carbohydrates	3.7g	3.7g
fibre	3.4g	3.4g
sodium	311mg	390mg

Seafood

Seafood is low in both total and saturated fats and provides substantial B vitamins as well as being rich in many important minerals. All seafood, but in particular oil-rich fish such as salmon, contains healthy Omega-3 fatty acids which have beneficial cholesterol lowering effects. As a result of these benefits seafood should be eaten at least twice per week.

Prawns with Pak Choi

Serves 4

INGREDIENTS

2 tablespoons soy sauce

2 garlic cloves, crushed

1 small red chilli, finely sliced

4 x 120g green king prawns, peeled, deveined,
tails intact (females)

4 x 220g green king prawns, peeled, deveined,
tails intact (males)

½ cup salt reduced fish stock

1 tablespoon oil

2 shallots, cut diagonally into 3cm lengths

1 bunch baby pak choi, halved

METHOD

1. Combine soy sauce, garlic, chilli and prawns.
Marinate for 30 minutes in the refrigerator.

2. Remove prawns from marinade. Reserve 2
tablespoons of the marinade and combine with
the stock and set aside.

3. Heat the oil in a wok until hot. Add and cook
half the prawns until they are coloured, remove
from wok. Repeat with the remaining prawns.

4. Add shallots and pak choi to wok and stir fry
for 1 minute. Return prawns and stock mixture
to the wok and cook for 1-2 minutes until the
sauce thickens. Serve immediately garnished
with extra shallots.

PER SERVING

AVERAGE QUANTITY	FEMALES	MALES
energy	201cal	302cal
protein	30g	53.4g
fat / saturated	7.6g / 1.4g	8.3g / 1.5g
cholesterol	204mg	373mg
carbohydrates	1.9g	1.9g
fibre	1.4g	1.4g
sodium	944mg	1342mg

Chilli & Lime Salmon with Thai Herb Salad

Serves 4

INGREDIENTS

Juice from 1 lime
1 clove garlic, crushed
2 tablespoons soy sauce
1 small red chilli, finely chopped
2 tablespoons olive oil
4 x 120g salmon fillets (females)
4 x 220g salmon fillets (males)

THAI HERB SALAD

1 cucumber, halved lengthways, seeds removed and sliced thinly
150g cherry tomatoes, halved
½ cup loosely packed basil leaves
½ cup loosely packed mint leaves
½ cup loosely packed coriander
1 cup bean sprouts
1 tablespoon lime juice
1 teaspoon olive oil
1 teaspoon soy sauce
Chopped red chilli (optional)

METHOD

1. In a large bowl combine lime juice, garlic, soy sauce, chilli and 1 tablespoon of the oil. Mix with a fork. Place salmon fillets in the bowl and coat thoroughly in the marinade. Set aside for 30 minutes in the fridge.
2. Heat remaining oil in a large frying pan on high. Cook salmon until golden and crispy on the outside but pink on the inside.
3. Combine all salad ingredients in a large bowl and toss to combine. Serve salmon on top of salad with extra chilli on top if desired. Drizzle any extra dressing over salmon.

Tip: Salmon is a rich source of Omega-3 fatty acids and is one of the healthiest forms of protein. These fats are essential for good health and they cannot be made within the body. Their benefits include; controlling cholesterol levels, improving digestion and increasing the body's ability to burn fat.

PER SERVING

AVERAGE QUANTITY	FEMALES	MALES
energy	367cal	551cal
protein	32.3g	57.5g
fat / saturated	24.8g / 4.5g	34g / 6.6g
cholesterol	82mg	150mg
carbohydrates	2.4g	2.4g
fibre	1.9g	1.9g
sodium	492mg	551mg

Pan Fried Fish with Herbs

Serves 4

INGREDIENTS

4 tablespoons olive oil
1 clove garlic, crushed
1 tablespoon chives, chopped
1 tablespoon dill, chopped
1 tablespoon thyme, chopped
2 tablespoons lemon juice
2 shallots, chopped
Ground black pepper
4 x 120g firm white fish fillets (females)
4 x 220g firm white fish fillets (males)
2 bunches broccolini, trimmed and cut into thirds
4 button squash, quartered (optional)
Lemon wedges to serve

METHOD

1. Combine half the oil, garlic, fresh herbs, lemon juice, shallots and pepper in a small bowl. Coat the fish fillets in the herb mixture.
2. Heat the remaining oil in a large frying pan over high heat. Cook fish fillets until golden brown.
3. Serve fish with steamed broccolini, squash and a squeeze of lemon juice with ground pepper.

PER SERVING

AVERAGE QUANTITY	FEMALES	MALES
energy	344cal	468cal
protein	33g	57.5g
fat / saturated	21.8g / 3.7g	24.6g / 4.5g
cholesterol	92mg	169mg
carbohydrates	2.1g	2.1g
fibre	3.3g	3.3g
sodium	148mg	261mg

Wok Fried Scallops

Serves 4

INGREDIENTS

2 tablespoons soy sauce
1 teaspoon sesame oil
4 x 120g scallops (females)
4 x 220g scallops (males)
2 tablespoons fish sauce
½ cup water
Olive oil spray
2cm piece of ginger, peeled and thinly shredded
1 clove garlic, thinly shredded
400g mange tout, trimmed and thinly shredded
2 shallots, thinly shredded diagonally
1 red pepper, seeded and thinly sliced

METHOD

1. Remove scallops from shell.
2. Mix half the soy sauce, sesame oil and scallops in a bowl. Toss.
3. In a second bowl combine fish sauce, water and the remaining soy sauce. Set aside.
4. Heat a wok on high, spray with olive oil and stir fry half the scallops until cooked. Remove and repeat with remaining scallops.
5. Wipe wok clean and add ginger, garlic, mange tout, shallots and the red pepper. Stir fry for 2 minutes. Add reserved fish sauce mixture and bring to boil.
6. Add scallops back to pan until warmed then serve.

PER SERVING

AVERAGE QUANTITY	FEMALES	MALES
energy	208cal	301cal
protein	28g	47.4g
fat / saturated	6.3g / <1g	7.5g / <1g
cholesterol	66mg	121mg
carbohydrates	7.9g	7.9g
fibre	3g	3g
sodium	1613mg	1885mg

Ginger & Soy Calamari

Serves 4

INGREDIENTS

480g squid hoods (females)
880g squid hoods (males)
2 tablespoons fish sauce
1 teaspoon soy sauce
2 tablespoons lime juice
3cm piece of ginger, peeled, finely grated
¼ cup coriander leaves, chopped
Olive oil spray
1 small mango
150g baby rocket leaves
Lime wedges to serve

METHOD

1. Slice squid hoods, open flat and score the inside with a sharp knife in a diamond pattern. Cut into 3cm pieces.
2. Combine sauces, lime juice, ginger and coriander in a small bowl. Whisk with a fork. Add calamari and toss to coat. Cover and refrigerate for 30 minutes.
3. Remove calamari from marinade. Pour marinade into a small saucepan. Bring to the boil over high heat. Reduce heat to medium and simmer for 3 minutes.
4. Preheat barbecue to high heat. Spray with olive oil. Cook half the calamari score side down for 1 minute. Turn and cook for a further minute or until tender. Repeat with the remaining calamari.
5. Cut mango into cubes and char lightly on a barbecue. Divide rocket between plates, top with calamari, mango and drizzle with warm dressing and a squeeze of lime juice.

PER SERVING

AVERAGE QUANTITY	FEMALES	MALES
energy	201cal	332cal
protein	35.8g	63.6g
fat / saturated	3.7g / <1g	5.7g / 1.5g
cholesterol	398mg	730mg
carbohydrates	4.8g	4.8g
fibre	1g	1g
sodium	1681mg	2155mg

Paprika Spiced Bream with Salsa

Serves 4

INGREDIENTS

4 x 120g bream fillets (females)
4 x 220g bream fillets (males)
1 tablespoon ground cumin
½ teaspoon paprika
1 clove garlic, crushed
2 tablespoons olive oil
100g green beans

SALSA

1 cucumber, diced
2 tomatoes, finely diced
½ Spanish onion, finely diced
2 tablespoons coriander leaves, chopped
1 tablespoon balsamic vinegar

METHOD

1. Place fish fillets into shallow baking tray. Combine cumin, paprika, garlic and oil to form a paste. Rub over the fish. Set aside for 20 minutes.
2. Preheat barbecue plate to high. Reduce heat to medium and spray with olive oil. Cook fish for 3 minutes each side, or until cooked through.
3. Steam beans until tender.
4. Combine all salsa ingredients in a bowl and toss to combine.
5. Serve fish with salsa and green beans.

PER SERVING

AVERAGE QUANTITY	FEMALES	MALES
energy	301cal	463cal
protein	32g	57.4g
fat / saturated	17.2g / 4g	23.8g / 6.3g
cholesterol	115mg	211mg
carbohydrates	3.4g	3.4g
fibre	2.2g	2.2g
sodium	143mg	252mg

Barbecued Prawns Serves 4

INGREDIENTS

2 tablespoons fresh lemon juice
1 tablespoon fish sauce
2 tablespoons olive oil
4 kaffir lime leaves, chopped finely
2 cloves garlic, chopped finely
1 red chilli, seeded, thinly sliced

4 x 120g large king prawns, peeled,
   deveined with tail and head intact (females)
4 x 220g large king prawns, peeled,
   deveined with tail and head intact (males)
2 tablespoons coriander, roughly chopped
Lemon wedges to serve

METHOD

1. Combine lemon juice, fish sauce, oil, lime leaves, garlic and chilli in a large glass bowl. Add prawns and toss.
2. Heat barbecue or char grill to high and cook prawns in batches, brushing with marinade as they cook. Cook for 2-3 minutes each side until they change colour, curl up and the shells turn brown.
3. Sprinkle with coriander and a squeeze of lemon juice.

Serving suggestion: Serve with a fresh garden salad.

PER SERVING

AVERAGE QUANTITY	FEMALES	MALES
energy	210cal	311cal
protein	28.6g	51.9g
fat / saturated	10g / 1.4g	10.7g / 1.5g
cholesterol	203mg	372mg
carbohydrates	<1g	<1g
fibre	<1g	<1g
sodium	936mg	1334mg

Vegetarian

Tofu and other soy-based products are relatively high in protein and good fats. They are cholesterol free which makes them an ideal protein source. Eggs are also a good choice as they are relatively low in calories and saturated fat. The protein contained in eggs is a complete source, which means it is easily absorbed by the body. Just make sure you limit eggs to 6 per week.

Tofu Kebabs

Serves 4

INGREDIENTS

8 skewers
4 x 150g firm tofu, cut into cubes (females)
4 x 250g firm tofu, cut into cubes (males)
1 large green pepper, seeded and cut into cubes
2 small courgettes, sliced
4 button squash, halved (optional)
100g button mushrooms, halved
2 tablespoons soy sauce
2 tablespoons sesame oil
2 teaspoons grated ginger
1 clove garlic, crushed
1 small chilli, chopped finely

METHOD

1. Thread the tofu and vegetables alternately onto the skewers. Lay in a large baking dish in a single layer.
2. Combine remaining ingredients in a small bowl to make a paste. Pour over the kebabs and set aside for 30 minutes to allow flavours to develop.
3. Cook skewers on a hot barbecue or grill plate basting as they cook for 10-15 minutes until tofu is browned.

Serving suggestion: Serve with a side salad.

PER SERVING

AVERAGE QUANTITY	FEMALES	MALES
energy	224cal	297cal
protein	15.1g	23.2g
fat / saturated	16.1g / 2.3g	20.3g / 2.9g
cholesterol	<1mg	<1mg
carbohydrates	3.8g	4.4g
fibre	2.9g	3.2g
sodium	12mg	16mg

Grilled Vegetable Stack Serves 4

IINGREDIENTS

Olive oil spray
1 large aubergine, sliced lengthways
1 red pepper, seeded and quartered
2 large courgettes, sliced lengthways
4 large flat mushrooms, stems removed
1 Spanish onion, thickly sliced
4 × 150g low fat ricotta cheese (females)

4 × 200g low fat ricotta cheese (males)
2 cloves garlic, sliced
½ cup fresh basil, chopped
2 tablespoons fresh chives, finely chopped
Balsamic vinegar
Ground pepper

METHOD

1. Spray aubergine, red pepper, courgettes, mushrooms and onion with oil and cook in batches on a heated barbecue or grill plate until tender.
2. Combine cheese, garlic and herbs in a medium bowl. Mix gently.
3. Divide the aubergine slices among serving plates. Layer with cheese mixture, courgettes, red pepper and mushroom. Top with another layer of cream cheese and onion.
4. Drizzle with balsamic vinegar and ground pepper.

PER SERVING

AVERAGE QUANTITY	FEMALES	MALES
energy	282cal	345cal
protein	20.5g	25.7g
fat / saturated	15.1g / 8.5g	19.5g / 11.3g
cholesterol	63mg	84mg
carbohydrates	12.6g	13.7g
fibre	7.1g	7.1g
sodium	294mg	387 mg

Curried Sausages Serves 4

INGREDIENTS

Olive oil spray
4 x 120g vegetarian sausages, sliced (females)*
4 x 220g vegetarian sausages, sliced (males)*
1 brown onion, sliced thinly
1 clove garlic, thinly sliced
1 tablespoon curry powder

1 teaspoon mustard powder
1 green pepper, seeded and diced thinly
1 carrot, peeled and sliced
1 cup mushrooms, sliced
1½ cups salt reduced vegetable stock
75g low fat smooth ricotta cheese
1 cup green beans, trimmed and cut into thirds

METHOD

1. Heat a large pan on high and spray with olive oil. Add sausages, onion, garlic, curry powder and mustard. Cook stirring continuously until sausages are starting to colour.
2. Add the green pepper, carrot and mushrooms and cook for 5 minutes.
3. Add stock and bring to the boil. Reduce heat to medium, add the ricotta and simmer for 10-15 minutes. Add beans, cook for a further 10 minutes and serve immediately.

PER SERVING

AVERAGE QUANTITY	FEMALES	MALES
energy	292cal	462cal
protein	27g	44.8g
fat / saturated	13.4g / 2.8g	21.3g / 4g
cholesterol	8mg	8mg
carbohydrates	13.5g	19.6g
fibre	6.1g	8.2g
sodium	998mg	1456mg

*When using packaged goods check the nutrition label. It must be under 5g carbohydrates per serving.

Courgette & Ricotta Frittata

Serves 4

INGREDIENTS

4 eggs
4 egg whites, separated
2 cloves garlic, crushed
2 large courgettes, coarsely grated
200g reduced fat ricotta cheese, loosely crumbled
Salt and pepper
2 teaspoons oil
1 punnet cherry tomatoes, halved
½ cup small basil leaves, loosely packed

METHOD

1. Preheat grill to high.
2. Whisk eggs, egg whites and garlic in a bowl. Gently fold in courgettes and ricotta and season with salt and pepper.
3. Heat oil in a 20cm diameter frying pan (with metal handle) over medium heat. Pour in courgette mixture and cook for 5-6 minutes until just set around the edges but still runny in the middle.
4. Remove from the heat and place under the grill about 6cm from the heat source for 2-3 minutes until golden brown and just set. Remove from the grill.
5. Cut into wedges. Serve 1 wedge for a female and 2 wedges for a male. Serve frittata with cherry tomatoes sprinkled with basil leaves and freshly ground black pepper.

PER SERVING

AVERAGE QUANTITY	FEMALES	MALES
energy	194cal	424cal
protein	13.4g	26.8g
fat / saturated	13.1g / 5g	26.2g / 9.9g
cholesterol	236mg	492mg
carbohydrates	4.4g	8.8g
fibre	2.8g	5.6g
sodium	163mg	465mg

Vegetarian San Choy Bow

Serves 4

INGREDIENTS

1 tablespoon olive oil
2 cloves garlic, crushed
1 small onion, finely chopped
4 x 150g firm tofu, finely diced (females)
4 x 250g firm tofu, finely diced (males)
2 teaspoons finely grated fresh ginger
1 red pepper, seeded, diced
2 shallots, ends trimmed, finely chopped
2 tablespoons fish sauce
2 tablespoons soy sauce
100g bean sprouts
8 large iceberg lettuce leaves, washed and dried
Chopped coriander to garnish

METHOD

1. Heat oil in wok on high heat.
2. Add garlic and onion and stir fry until soft. Add tofu, ginger, red pepper and stir fry for 2 minutes. Add shallots and sauces and cook for 3 minutes.
3. Remove from heat and add bean sprouts, stir until just wilted.
4. Spoon into lettuce cups and garnish with chopped coriander.

PER SERVING

AVERAGE QUANTITY	FEMALES	MALES
energy	185cal	259cal
protein	15.4g	23.5g
fat / saturated	11.2g / 1.6g	15.4g / 2.2g
cholesterol	-	-
carbohydrates	4.2g	4.8g
fibre	2.7g	3g
sodium	1300mg	1304mg

Stuffed Peppers

Serves 4

INGREDIENTS

1 tablespoon olive oil
1 onion, chopped finely
1 clove garlic, crushed
2 courgettes, grated
400g can crushed tomatoes
2 tablespoons balsamic vinegar
1 tablespoon oregano, chopped finely
1 tablespoon marjoram
4 large red peppers
4 x 150g low fat ricotta cheese (females)
4 x 200g low fat ricotta cheese (males)

METHOD

1. Preheat oven to 180°C.
2. Heat oil in a large frying pan and cook onion
and garlic until soft. Add courgettes and tomatoes,
breaking them up with a wooden spoon. Bring to
the boil. Reduce heat and simmer for 10 minutes
until sauce is thickened.
3. Add balsamic vinegar and herbs and mix gently.
Remove from heat.
4. Slice the top off each pepper and reserve.
Remove the seeds and core. Stand the peppers up
in the base of a baking tray.
5. Half fill each pepper with the tomato mixture.
Add half the cheese into each pepper, followed
by the remaining tomato mixture and the rest of
the cheese. Replace the tops and bake for 25-30
minutes until peppers are softened.

*Serving suggestion: Serve on its own or with
a side salad.*

PER SERVING

AVERAGE QUANTITY	FEMALES	MALES
energy	300cal	364cal
protein	19.4g	24.6g
fat / saturated	18.3g / 9g	22.6g / 11.4g
cholesterol	63mg	84mg
carbohydrates	12.4g	13.5g
fibre	4.3g	4.3g
sodium	297mg	390mg

Tofu, Courgette & Aubergine Stir Fry Serves 4

INGREDIENTS

1 tablespoon balsamic vinegar
2 cloves garlic, crushed
4 x 150g firm tofu cut into 2cm cubes (females)
4 x 250g firm tofu cut into 2cm cubes (males)
1 teaspoon olive oil
3 baby aubergines, thinly sliced, diagonally
2 courgettes, thinly sliced, diagonally
⅓ cup salt reduced vegetable stock
100g mange tout, trimmed

BASIL PESTO

1 cup firmly packed fresh basil
2 tablespoons olive oil
1 clove garlic, crushed
Salt and pepper
¼ cup salt reduced vegetable stock

METHOD

1. Place pesto ingredients in a food processor and process until smooth. Set aside.
2. Combine 1 tablespoon of the pesto, the balsamic vinegar and garlic in a large glass bowl. Add tofu and toss until well coated. Set aside for 30 minutes.
3. Heat half the oil in a wok over medium heat. Stir fry tofu for 5 minutes until lightly browned. Remove and return to pesto bowl and coat.
4. Heat the remaining oil in the wok on medium to high heat. Add aubergine and stir fry for 3 minutes. Add courgettes and cook for a further 2 minutes. Add stock and cook until the vegetables are tender.
5. Add tofu and remaining pesto and cook until heated through. Add mange tout and cook for 1 minute. Serve immediately.

PER SERVING

AVERAGE QUANTITY	FEMALES	MALES
energy	250cal	323cal
protein	14.7g	22.8g
fat / saturated	17.6g / 2.4g	21.7g / 3g
cholesterol	-	-
carbohydrates	6.5g	7g
fibre	4.4g	4.7g
sodium	202mg	206mg

Side Dishes

Vegetables are an essential source of vitamins, minerals and dietary fibre and because they are low in energy they can be eaten in unlimited amounts. They are fantastic in stir fries, soups and eaten raw to fill you up throughout the day. Keep them interesting by experimenting with different flavours and ways of cooking them.

Stir Fried Vegetables Serves 4

INGREDIENTS

Olive oil spray
1 teaspoon crushed garlic
1 medium red chilli, chopped
1 teaspoon ginger grated
½ red pepper, thinly sliced
½ yellow pepper, thinly sliced
2 button squash, quartered (optional)

1 courgette, chopped into batons
1 cup broccoli florets
1 cup cauliflower florets
1 carrot, sliced into matchsticks
2 shallots, sliced diagonally
150g green beans, trimmed, halved
3 tablespoons soy sauce

METHOD

1. Heat a wok or large frying pan over high heat and spray lightly with olive oil.
2. Stir fry garlic, chilli and ginger for 1-2 minutes.
3. Add all vegetables, except for the beans and cook until tender.
4. Add beans and stir through the soy sauce, cook for 2 minutes then serve.

PER SERVING

AVERAGE QUANTITY	PER SERVING
energy	74cal
protein	5.3g
fat / saturated	1.5g / <1g
cholesterol	-
carbohydrates	6.7g
fibre	5.3g
sodium	571mg

Notatoes Mashed Potato Substitute | Serves 4 (¾ cup per serving)

INGREDIENTS

1 medium head cauliflower, cut into florets
75g light cream cheese
1 clove garlic, crushed

Salt and pepper to taste
Chives, chopped

METHOD

1. Steam cauliflower until tender.
2. Place in a blender or food processor with the cream cheese, garlic and salt and pepper.
3. Process until smooth.
4. Garnish with chopped chives and ground pepper.
Note: if the mixture is too thick try adding a small amount of salt reduced stock while blending.

PER SERVING

AVERAGE QUANTITY	PER SERVING
energy	55cal
protein	5.3g
fat / saturated	1.5g / <1g
cholesterol	-
carbohydrates	6.7g
fibre	5.3g
sodium	571mg

Cauliflower Rice

Serves 4

INGREDIENTS
500g cauliflower (1 medium head)
1 tablespoon olive oil
1 clove garlic, crushed
2 shallots, thinly sliced
1 tablespoon soy sauce (optional)
Salt and pepper

METHOD
1. Process the cauliflower, including the core in a food processor (or grate) until crumbly.
2. Heat oil in a large frying pan until hot, sauté garlic and shallots until tender. Add cauliflower and cook, stirring until golden brown.
3. Add soy sauce (optional) and salt and pepper to serve.

Tip: Great with curries and stir fries.

PER SERVING

AVERAGE QUANTITY	PER SERVING
energy	74cal
protein	3.2g
fat / saturated	4.8g / <1g
cholesterol	-
carbohydrates	3.1g
fibre	2.5g
sodium	208mg

Warm Tomato & Apple Salad

Serves 4

INGREDIENTS
1 punnet cherry tomatoes, halved
1 medium red chilli, finely diced
2 cloves garlic, crushed
2 medium Spanish onions, sliced
12 asparagus spears, trimmed and halved
2 tablespoons white wine vinegar
2 tablespoons lemon juice
½ cup mint leaves
200g rocket
1 green apple, cut into thin wedges

METHOD
1. Heat wok on high heat and lightly spray with olive oil. Add tomatoes, chilli, garlic, onion and cook for 5 minutes until softened, stirring continuously.
2. Add asparagus, white wine vinegar, lemon and 1 teaspoon of mint, cook for 5 minutes.
3. Place rocket in a large bowl. Add tomato, asparagus mixture and toss. Serve sprinkled with fresh mint and apple wedges.

PER SERVING

AVERAGE QUANTITY	PER SERVING
energy	72cal
protein	4.1g
fat / saturated	<1g / <1g
cholesterol	-
carbohydrates	9.6g
fibre	4.4g
sodium	29mg

Roast Vegetables Serves 4

INGREDIENTS

2 red peppers, seeded and quartered
1 aubergine cut into long wedges
2 courgettes, halved and sliced lengthways
1 carrot peeled, halved, sliced lengthways
6 asparagus spears, halved

2 tablespoons olive oil
1 clove garlic, crushed
Salt and pepper
1 cup cherry tomatoes

METHOD

1. Preheat oven to 200°C.
2. Combine all ingredients except the cherry tomatoes in a large baking dish lined with baking paper and toss to coat in the oil.
3. Roast for 30-35 minutes until vegetables are tender.
4. Remove from the oven, add the cherry tomatoes and increase oven temperature to 230°C. Roast the vegetables for a further 5-7 minutes until well coloured.

PER SERVING

AVERAGE QUANTITY	PER SERVING
energy	156cal
protein	4g
fat / saturated	9.9g / 1.3g
cholesterol	-
carbohydrates	9.3g
fibre	6.4g
sodium	23mg

Garlic & Balsamic Mushrooms Serves 4

INGREDIENTS

2 cloves garlic, crushed
2 tablespoons balsamic vinegar
12 small flat mushrooms, stalks trimmed

Olive oil spray
¼ cup tarragon, chopped

METHOD

1. Combine garlic and vinegar in a small bowl.
Using a pastry brush, coat the tops of the mushrooms
with the mixture.
2. Place stalk side up on a baking tray and spray with
olive oil.
3. Grill under a hot grill for 4-5 minutes.
4. Serve sprinkled with fresh tarragon.

PER SERVING

AVERAGE QUANTITY	PER SERVING
energy	22cal
protein	1.4g
fat / saturated	1g / <1g
cholesterol	-
carbohydrates	<1g
fibre	1.2g
sodium	3mg

Roasted Tomatoes with Baby Spinach & Pesto

Serves 4

INGREDIENTS

8 ripe vine tomatoes, halved
1 tablespoon olive oil
2 cloves garlic, sliced
16 fresh basil leaves
100g baby spinach leaves

PESTO DRESSING

1 tablespoon olive oil
1 tablespoon balsamic vinegar
2 tablespoons basil pesto*

METHOD

1. Preheat oven to 200°C.
2. Place tomatoes, oil, garlic, basil and spinach in bowl. Toss to combine.
3. Line a baking tray with foil and place tomatoes cut side up on tray.
4. Sprinkle with garlic and basil leaves and roast for 35-40 minutes until the edges are shrivelled. Cool for 10 minutes.
5. Place spinach and tomatoes in a large bowl. Drizzle with pesto dressing and toss.

PESTO DRESSING

Place all ingredients in a jar and shake well.

PER SERVING

AVERAGE QUANTITY	PER SERVING
energy	180cal
protein	45g
fat / saturated	13.4g / 2.1g
cholesterol	2mg
carbohydrates	6.7g
fibre	5g
sodium	121mg

*When using packaged goods check the nutrition label. It must be under 5g carbohydrates per serving.

Spicy Char-grilled Asparagus

Serves 4

INGREDIENTS
2 tablespoons olive oil
1 tablespoon balsamic vinegar
1 teaspoon cumin
1 teaspoon coriander, chopped
1 clove garlic, crushed
2 bunches asparagus, woody ends removed
Lemon wedges

METHOD
1. Combine oil, balsamic vinegar, cumin, coriander and garlic in a bowl. Whisk together.
2. Place asparagus in a single layer in a shallow dish. Pour dressing over spears and turn to coat.
3. Heat the grill plate of a barbecue and cook asparagus until tender.
4. Serve drizzled with extra dressing and a squeeze of lemon.

PER SERVING

AVERAGE QUANTITY	PER SERVING
energy	92cal
protein	1.3g
fat / saturated	9.1g / 1.3g
cholesterol	-
carbohydrates	<1g
fibre	<1g
sodium	1mg

Garlic & Basil Beans

Serves 4

INGREDIENTS
100g green beans, trimmed and halved lengthways
1 tablespoon olive oil
1 clove garlic, crushed
1 tablespoon basil

METHOD
1. Blanch beans by plunging into boiling water and refreshing in iced water.
2. Heat oil in a medium frying pan.
3. Add garlic and beans and cook while stirring for 2-3 minutes. Stir in fresh basil leaves and serve.

PER SERVING

AVERAGE QUANTITY	PER SERVING
energy	47cal
protein	<1g
fat / saturated	4.6g / <1g
cholesterol	-
carbohydrates	<1g
fibre	<1g
sodium	<1mg

Mixed Green Salad with Harissa Dressing

Serves 4

INGREDIENTS

½ green oakleaf lettuce, washed and dried
50g watercress leaves
1 avocado, thinly sliced
1 cucumber, seeds removed, sliced
2 shallots, chopped

DRESSING

1 fresh long green chilli, chopped

2 shallots, chopped
1 clove of garlic, chopped
1 teaspoon ground coriander
1 teaspoon sweet paprika
¼ teaspoon ground tumeric
1 tablespoon lemon juice
1 tablespoon olive oil

METHOD

1. Tear oakleaf lettuce leaves roughly and place in a large bowl with watercress. Scatter with avocado, cucumber slices and shallots.
2. Divide between serving plates and drizzle with Harissa dressing.

DRESSING

1. Combine all ingredients, except oil in a mortar and pestle and grind until smooth. Add oil and pound to combine. Alternatively combine all ingredients in a small food processor and blend until smooth.

PER SERVING

AVERAGE QUANTITY	PER SERVING
energy	161cal
protein	2.5g
fat / saturated	15g / 2.9g
cholesterol	-
carbohydrates	2.8g
fibre	3.2g
sodium	38mg

Snacks

Having 2 to 3 small healthy snacks each day will
keep your energy levels stable between meals and
stop you from over-consuming at your main meals.
Fruit is one of the healthiest snacks you can choose,
especially those high in fibre and low in GI, like apples.
Other suitable snacks are diet jelly and raw vegetables
with a low calorie dip.

Baby Spinach Chips

INGREDIENTS

200g bag baby spinach
Mixed herbs

Salt and freshly ground black pepper to taste
Olive oil spray

METHOD

1. Place the baby spinach leaves in a single layer on a lightly oiled baking tray.
2. Sprinkle the leaves with the herbs, salt and pepper and spray lightly with olive oil.
3. Bake in a 180°C oven for 7 minutes or until crispy.
4. Ensure you store excess chips in an airtight container.

Tip: For a different flavour try adding lemon juice and black pepper, soy sauce or chilli and lime juice to the chips prior to baking.

PER SERVING

AVERAGE QUANTITY	PER 50G SERVING	PER 100G
energy	23cal	46cal
protein	1.5g	3g
fat / saturated	1.1g / <1g	2.2g / <1g
cholesterol	-	-
carbohydrates	<1g	<1g
fibre	1.3g	2.6g
sodium	25mg	50mg

Roast Aubergine Dip Serves 4

INGREDIENTS

2 medium aubergines
1 clove crushed garlic
2 teaspoons lemon juice
2 teaspoons olive oil
2 tablespoons flat leaf parsley, chopped finely

Salt and pepper to taste
½ teaspoon cumin
1 small chilli (optional)
1 tablespoon fresh parsley, chopped

METHOD

1. Prick the skin of the aubergines several times.
2. Cut in half and bake cut side down on a lightly greased baking tray for 30 minutes at 190°C.
3. Remove from the oven and discard the skins then blend in a food processor with all other remaining ingredients until smooth.
4. Garnish with parsley.

Serving suggestion: Serve with raw vegetable sticks such as carrot, celery, peppers and mange tout.

PER SERVING

AVERAGE QUANTITY	PER 120G SERVING	PER 100G
energy	38cal	31cal
protein	1.5g	1.2g
fat / saturated	1.3g / <1g	1.1g / <1g
cholesterol	-	-
carbohydrates	3.4g	2.9g
fibre	3g	2.5g
sodium	9mg	7mg

Spicy Cauliflower Popcorn

INGREDIENTS

2 cups cauliflower florets (200g)
Cajun seasoning

Salt and pepper to taste
Olive oil spray

METHOD

1. Place cauliflower in a large bowl with Cajun seasoning, salt and pepper and toss to coat.
2. Place onto an oiled baking tray and spray lightly with olive oil, adding extra seasoning if required.
3. Bake in a moderate oven (180°C) for 15-20 minutes or until golden.

Tip: For a different flavour try adding chilli, curry powder or any other spices.

PER SERVING

AVERAGE QUANTITY	PER 50G SERVING	PER 100G
energy	19cal	39cal
protein	1.1g	2.1g
fat / saturated	1g / <1g	2g / <1g
cholesterol	-	-
carbohydrates	1g	2g
fibre	<1g	1.8g
sodium	65mg	131mg

Guacamole

INGREDIENTS

1 ripe avocado
1 tablespoon of lime or lemon juice
1 red chilli, finely chopped

1 tablespoon coriander, finely chopped
1 teaspoon Tabasco sauce

METHOD

1. Remove avocado from its skin, chop flesh then mash with a fork. Add lime or lemon juice and mix.
2. Stir in the chilli, coriander and Tabasco sauce. Combine well with a fork.
3. Serve immediately or store covered in the fridge.

Serving suggestion: *Serve with raw vegetable sticks such as carrot, celery, peppers and mange tout.*

PER SERVING

AVERAGE QUANTITY	PER 60G SERVING	PER 100G
energy	113cal	188cal
protein	1g	1.8g
fat / saturated	11.8g / 2.6g	19.7g / 4.3g
cholesterol	-	-
carbohydrates	<1g	<1g
fibre	<1g	1.4g
sodium	8mg	13mg

Vegetable Soup

Serves 4

INGREDIENTS

1 small onion, diced
1 clove garlic, crushed
1 medium carrot, diced
2 celery stalks, thinly sliced
6 cups chicken stock
500g cauliflower, cut into florets
2 large courgettes, diced
150g green beans cut into thirds

METHOD

1. Heat a large pot on high. Spray with olive oil and add onion and garlic and cook till soft.
2. Add carrot and celery and cook stirring for 2 minutes.
3. Add stock, cauliflower and courgettes and bring to the boil.
4. Add beans, reduce heat and simmer for 10 minutes.

PER SERVING

AVERAGE QUANTITY	PER 300G SERVING	PER 100G
energy	79cal	16cal
protein	8g	1.6g
fat / saturated	<1g / <1g	<1g / <1g
cholesterol	-	-
carbohydrates	7.9g	1.6g
fibre	3.9g	<1g
sodium	813mg	163mg

Jelly Snakes

INGREDIENTS

1 sachet Tony Ferguson Simply Diet-Jelly
2 teaspoons gelatin
Water

METHOD

1. Make jelly according to instructions and add extra gelatin. Stir until dissolved.
2. Pour jelly into a 20x30cm (8x12in) rectangular cake tin or plastic container set in the refrigerator until firm.
3. Once set, cut into strips using a sharp knife and store in an airtight container in the fridge.

PER SERVING

AVERAGE QUANTITY	PER 125G SERVING	PER 100G
energy	16cal	13cal
protein	2.9g	2.3g
fat / saturated	<1g / <1g	<1g / <1g
cholesterol	-	-
carbohydrates	<1g	<1g
fibre	1.1g	<1g
sodium	35mg	27mg

Sauces &
Dressings

Healthy food need not be tasteless and boring.
Adding a small amount of dressing or sauce
to a meal or a salad can make all the difference.
Beware of supermarket products which are often
high in hidden fats, salt and energy and always make
sure they are less than 5g of carbohydrates per
serving. Try making your own; you can create any
flavour you like and you can be sure they will
be fresh and tasty!

Lemon Twist Dressing
Makes ⅓ cup

INGREDIENTS
2 tablespoons extra virgin olive oil
Juice from 1 medium lemon
1 teaspoon garlic, crushed
½ teaspoon oregano
Salt and ground black pepper to taste

METHOD
Shake all the ingredients together in a screw top jar until
well combined. Lasts for 2 to 3 days in the refrigerator.

*Tip: Add any other herbs and spices, mustard or sweetener
to vary the taste of the dressing.*

PER SERVING

AVERAGE QUANTITY	PER TABLESPOON	PER 100ML
energy	78cal	389cal
protein	<1g	<1g
fat / saturated	8.4g / 1.2g	42g / 5.9g
cholesterol	-	-
carbohydrates	<1g	1.7g
fibre	<1g	<1g
sodium	56mg	280mg

Red Wine & Garlic Marinade
Makes 3 cups

INGREDIENTS
½ cup water
2 cups red wine vinegar
½ cup Worcestershire sauce
1 clove garlic, crushed
1 teaspoon ginger
1 tablespoon fresh chives, chopped
1 tablespoon fresh basil, roughly chopped
Freshly ground black pepper

METHOD
Combine all ingredients in a screw top jar and shake to
combine. Place in the refrigerator for 1 hour prior to use
to allow flavours to develop.

PER SERVING

AVERAGE QUANTITY	PER 60G (¼ CUP)	PER 100ML
energy	17cal	29cal
protein	<1g	<1g
fat / saturated	<1g / <1g	<1g / <1g
cholesterol	-	-
carbohydrates	2.5g	4.1g
fibre	<1g	<1g
sodium	149mg	248mg

Chunky Tomato Salsa
Makes 2 cups

INGREDIENTS
1 Spanish onion, diced
1 clove garlic, chopped
4 tomatoes, quartered
2 tablespoons oregano, chopped
2 tablespoons basil, chopped

1 small avocado, diced
1 tablespoon lemon juice
½ tablespoon balsamic vinegar
Salt and pepper

METHOD
1. Combine all ingredients except for lemon juice,
vinegar, salt and pepper in a bowl and mix to combine.
2. Mix lemon juice, vinegar and seasoning in a bowl and
whisk with a fork.
3. Pour over salsa and toss gently.

PER SERVING

AVERAGE QUANTITY	PER 60G (¼ CUP)	PER 100G
energy	33cal	55cal
protein	<1g	1.2g
fat / saturated	2.6g / <1g	4.2g / <1g
cholesterol	-	-
carbohydrates	1.2g	2g
fibre	<1g	1.3g
sodium	18mg	31mg

Rosemary & Mint Dressing Makes 3 cups

INGREDIENTS
½ cup sweetener
1 cup water
1 cup malt vinegar
½ cup mint leaves, chopped finely
½ cup rosemary leaves, chopped finely

METHOD
1. Put the sweetener in a pan with 1 cup of water.
Stir over low heat without boiling, until dissolved.
2. Bring to the boil, reduce the heat and simmer for
3 minutes without stirring. Remove from heat.
3. Combine with vinegar, mint and rosemary. Cover, leave
for 10-20 minutes for flavours to develop before serving.

PER SERVING

AVERAGE QUANTITY	PER TABLESPOON	PER 100ML
energy	7cal	35cal
protein	<1g	<1g
fat / saturated	<1g / <1g	<1g / <1g
cholesterol	-	-
carbohydrates	<1g	4.6g
fibre	<1g	<1g
sodium	1mg	7mg

Soy & Ginger Dressing Makes 1 cup

INGREDIENTS
½ cup light soy sauce
2 teaspoons finely grated ginger
2 teaspoons rice wine vinegar
¼ teaspoon sweetener
1 shallot, end trimmed and finely chopped
1 small red chilli, seeded and finely chopped
2 teaspoons fresh lime juice

METHOD
Combine all ingredients in a small bowl and mix until
sweetener is dissolved.

PER SERVING

AVERAGE QUANTITY	PER TABLESPOON	PER 100ML
energy	7cal	35cal
protein	<1g	4.3g
fat / saturated	<1g / <0g	<1g / 0g
cholesterol	-	-
carbohydrates	<1g	2.7g
fibre	<1g	<1g
sodium	519mg	2597mg

Tomato Pasta Sauce Makes 3 cups

INGREDIENTS
2 kg ripe tomatoes
1 tablespoon olive oil
2 large onions, finely chopped
2 cloves garlic, crushed

4 tablespoons tomato pureé
1 tablespoon fresh oregano, chopped
1½ teaspoons sweetener

METHOD
1. Make a cross on the base of each tomato, place the
tomatoes in a bowl of boiling water for 10 seconds,
then put in cold water and peel off the skin from the
cross. Finely chop the flesh.
2. Heat the oil in a pan on medium heat. Add onion
and cook for 3 minutes or until onions are soft, stirring
continuously. Add garlic and cook for 1 minute.
3. Add tomato, tomato pureé, oregano and sweetener.
Bring to the boil, reduce heat and simmer for 20 minutes
or until the sauce has thickened slightly. Season to taste.

PER SERVING

AVERAGE QUANTITY	PER 60G (¼ CUP)	PER 100ML
energy	18cal	30cal
protein	<1g	1.3g
fat / saturated	<1g / <1g	<1g / <1g
cholesterol	<1g	<1g
carbohydrates	1.6g	2.7g
fibre	<1g	1.6g
sodium	5mg	9mg

Oil-Free Italian Dressing

Makes 2/3 cup

INGREDIENTS
¼ cup red wine vinegar
½ teaspoon Dijon mustard
¼ teaspoon sweetener
2 teaspoons water
Salt and freshly ground black pepper

METHOD
Add all ingredients to a screw top jar and shake to combine.

PER SERVING

AVERAGE QUANTITY	PER TABLESPOON	PER 100ML
energy	3cal	18cal
protein	<1g	<1g
fat / saturated	<1g / <1g	<1g / <1g
cholesterol	-	-
carbohydrates	<1g	<1g
fibre	<1g	<1g
sodium	81mg	406mg

Balsamic & Lime Dressing
Makes ⅔ cup

INGREDIENTS
2 tablespoons virgin olive oil
2 tablespoons lime juice
2 teaspoons balsamic vinegar
½ small red chilli, chopped finely
2 teaspoons soy sauce

METHOD
Shake all the ingredients together in a screw top jar until well combined.

PER SERVING

AVERAGE QUANTITY	PER TABLESPOON	PER 100ML
energy	51cal	256cal
protein	<1g	<1g
fat / saturated	5.4g / <1g	27g / 3.8g
cholesterol	-	-
carbohydrates	<1g	<1g
fibre	<1g	<1g
sodium	55mg	276mg

French Dressing

Makes ½ cup

INGREDIENTS
2 teaspoons white wine vinegar
1 tablespoon Dijon mustard
½ teaspoon sea salt
¼ teaspoon sweetener
½ cup olive oil

METHOD
1. Add all ingredients except the oil in a bowl and whisk to combine.
2. Add the oil in a steady stream while whisking until thick.
3. Season with salt and pepper.

PER SERVING

AVERAGE QUANTITY	PER TABLESPOON	PER 100ML
energy	147cal	736cal
protein	<1g	<1g
fat / saturated	16.5g / 2.3g	82.5g / 11.6g
cholesterol	<1mg	<1mg
carbohydrates	<1g	<1g
fibre	<1g	<1g
sodium	198mg	991mg

Balsamic Dressing

Makes ½ cup

INGREDIENTS
4 tablespoons extra virgin olive oil
2½ tablespoons balsamic vinegar
1 clove garlic, crushed
Pinch sweetener
Salt and pepper

METHOD
Add all ingredients to a screw top jar and shake to combine. Season with salt and pepper.

PER SERVING

AVERAGE QUANTITY	PER TABLESPOON	PER 100ML
energy	104cal	519cal
protein	<1g	<1g
fat / saturated	11.5g / 1.6g	57.5g / 8.1g
cholesterol	-	-
carbohydrates	<1g	<1g
fibre	<1g	<1g
sodium	<1mg	2mg

Index

Asian pork salad..................... 46

Asparagus, spicy char-grilled..... 81

Aubergine dip, roast............... 85

Aubergine, tofu & courgette
  stir fry................................... 70

Avocado salad, Cajun chicken... 32

Baby spinach chips................. 84

Balsamic dressing................... 94

Balsamic & lime dressing......... 94

Balsamic chicken................... 30

Balsamic lamb with
  asparagus salad.................... 35

Barbecued prawns................. 58

Beans, garlic & basil............... 81

Beef, Moroccan minted........... 11

Burritos.............................. 11

Cabbage salad, crunchy
  with lemon spiced chicken.... 23

Cajun chicken & avocado
  salad.................................. 32

Calamari, ginger soy............... 55

Cauliflower rice..................... 74

Cauliflower popcorn.............. 86

Chicken coriander................. 26

Chicken, lemon spice with
  crunchy cabbage salad.......... 23

Chicken, schnitzel................. 29

Chicken skewers, spiced.......... 27

Chicken with oven roasted
  tomatoes............................. 30

Chilli lime salmon with
  Thai herb salad.................... 51

Courgette & ricotta frittata...... 65

Creamy coconut curry............. 25

Curried sausages................... 63

Curry, creamy coconut............ 25

Curry, rich beef..................... 19

Fish, pan fried with herbs........ 52

French dressing..................... 94

Frittata, courgette & ricotta..... 65

Garlic & balsamic mushrooms... 77

Garlic & basil beans............... 81

Ginger soy calamari............... 55

Grilled vegetable stack........... 62

Guacamole........................... 87

Hearty Beef Casserole........... 15

Jelly snakes......................... 90

Lamb & mint salad................ 40

Lamb steaks, rosemary
  with ratatouille................... 39

Lemon garlic lamb rack.......... 37

Lemon sage pork cutlets......... 42

Lemon spice chicken with
  crunchy cabbage salad.......... 23

Lemon twist dressing............. 92

Marinade, red wine
  and garlic........................... 92

Meatballs, spicy.................... 20

Mixed green salad with
  Harissa dressing.................. 82

Moroccan minted beef............ 11

Mustard pork with warm
  tomato salad........................ 45

Notatoes.............................. 73

Oil-free Italian dressing........... 94

Pan fried fish with herbs......... 52

Paprika spiced bream
  with salsa........................... 57

Peppers, stuffed.................... 69

Pork chops with char-grilled
  vegetable salad.................... 43

Pork cutlets, lemon sage......... 42

Prawns & pak choi................. 49

Prawns, barbecued................ 58

Ratatouille, rosemary
  lamb steaks......................... 39

Red wine & garlic marinade..... 92

Rich beef curry..................... 19

Roast aubergine dip............... 85

Roast tomatoes with baby
  spinach & pesto................... 79

Roast vegetables................... 76

Rosemary & mint dressing....... 93

Rosemary lamb steaks
  with ratatouille................... 39

Sausages, curried.................. 63

Scallops, wok fried................ 52

Shepherd's pie...................... 17

Simply chicken schnitzel.......... 29

Soup, vegetable.................... 89

Soy & ginger dressing............. 93

Spiced chicken skewers........... 27

Spicy char-grilled asparagus..... 81

Spicy meatballs.................... 20

Spinach, chips...................... 84

Steak & onion salsa............... 13

Steak sandwich.................... 14

Stir fried vegetables.............. 72

Stuffed peppers.................... 69

Tofu kebabs......................... 61

Tofu, courgette & aubergine
  stir fry................................ 70

Tomato & apple salad,
  warm.................................. 74

Tomatoes, roast with baby
  spinach & pesto................... 79

Tomato pasta sauce............... 93

Tomato salsa....................... 92

Vegetable soup..................... 89

Vegetable stir fry.................. 72

Vegetarian san choy bow........ 67

Warm tomato & apple
  salad.................................. 74

Wok fried scallops................. 52

Conversion Chart

MEASURES

1 Australian metric measuring cup holds 250ml approximately; 1 Australian metric tablespoon holds 20ml; 1 Australian metric teaspoon holds 5ml.

Differences between measuring cups per country are within a 2 or 3 teaspoon variance, and will not affect your cooking results. North America, NZ and the UK use a 15ml tablespoon.

All cup and spoon measurements are level. The most accurate way of measuring dry ingredients is to weigh them. When measuring liquids use a clear glass or plastic jug with the metric markings.

LIQUID MEASURES

METRIC	IMPERIAL
30ml	1 fluid oz
60ml	2 fluid oz
100ml	3 fluid oz
125ml	4 fluid oz
150ml	5 fluid oz (¼pint, 1 gill)
190ml	6 fluid oz
250ml	8 fluid oz
300ml	10 fluid oz (½pint)
500ml	16 fluid oz
600ml	20 fluid oz (1 pint)
1000ml (1 litre)	1¾ pints

DRY MEASURES

METRIC	IMPERIAL
15g	½oz
30g	1oz
60g	2oz
125g	4oz (¼lb)
155g	5oz
185g	6oz
220g	7oz
250g	8oz (½lb)
280g	9oz
315g	10oz
345g	11oz
375g	12oz (¾lb)
410g	13oz
470g	15oz
500g	16oz (1lb)
750g	24oz (1½ lb)
1kg	32oz (2lb)

LENGTH MEASURES

METRIC	IMPERIAL
3mm	⅛in
6mm	¼in
1cm	½in
2cm	¾in
2.5cm	1in
5cm	2in
6cm	2½in
8cm	3in
10cm	4in
13cm	5in
15cm	6in
18cm	7in
20cm	8in
23cm	9in
25cm	10in
28cm	11in
30cm	12in (1ft)

OVEN TEMPERATURES

Oven temperatures are a guide for conventional ovens. For fan ovens, check the manufacturer's manual.

HEAT	°C (CELSIUS)	°F (FAHRENHEIT)	GAS MARK
Very slow	120	250	½
Slow	150	275-300	1-2
Moderately slow	170	325	3
Moderate	180	350-375	4-5
Moderately hot	200	400	6
Hot	220	425-450	7-8
Very hot	240	475	9